# TRUE BLUE

*poems by*

# Susan Scheid

*Finishing Line Press*
Georgetown, Kentucky

# TRUE BLUE

Copyright © 2025 by Susan Scheid
ISBN 979-8-89990-204-8 First Edition
All rights reserved under International and Pan-American Copyright Conventions. No part of this book may be reproduced in any manner whatsoever without written permission from the publisher, except in the case of brief quotations embodied in critical articles and reviews.

Publisher: Leah Huete de Maines
Editor: Christen Kincaid
Cover Art: Kassim Okusaga
Author Photo: Joe Meyer
Cover Design: Elizabeth Maines McCleavy

Order online: www.finishinglinepress.com
also available on amazon.com

Author inquiries and mail orders:
Finishing Line Press
PO Box 1626
Georgetown, Kentucky 40324
USA

# Contents

## I

Elegy for Pre-pandemic Existence .................................................. 1
the fragrance of your ancestors......................................................... 2
Ode to My Grandma's Kitchen Table .................................................. 3
Driving Home ........................................................................................ 4
Anniversary ........................................................................................... 5
Letter to My Mother in Her Absence .................................................. 6
Family Recipe ........................................................................................ 7
Not Even the Rain ................................................................................. 8
Ode to My Older Sister ........................................................................ 9
Birthday Poem #26 (for Sam) ............................................................ 10
Journey ................................................................................................. 11
Brotherly Love ..................................................................................... 12
Art Therapy .......................................................................................... 13

## II

Sovereignty .......................................................................................... 17
[what is the difference] ...................................................................... 18
Reflection ............................................................................................. 19
Ode to Dead Skin Cells ....................................................................... 20
The Jade Belt ....................................................................................... 21
Feral ..................................................................................................... 22
Juggling Scimitars ............................................................................... 23
Chaos Theory ...................................................................................... 24
The Weight of It All ............................................................................ 25
Anniversary Poem .............................................................................. 26
Bad Habits ........................................................................................... 27
from the ashes .................................................................................... 28
Self Portrait in 10 Lines ..................................................................... 29
Jean Cocteau's Orpheus ..................................................................... 30
Chaos .................................................................................................... 31
Grace .................................................................................................... 32
[where is the difference] .................................................................... 33
Poem With a Line from Sherwin Bitsui ............................................ 34
Blue Friday or the Bluest Blue ........................................................... 35
Resilience ............................................................................................. 37

Catharsis .................................................................................................. 38
The Sun is an Insomniac............................................................................ 39
Life is Beautiful ......................................................................................... 40
Beeswax...................................................................................................... 41
The Way ..................................................................................................... 42

## III

In Praise of the Vaccine ............................................................................ 45
Chaos II...................................................................................................... 46
Enter and Exit Singing .............................................................................. 47
Awakening.................................................................................................. 49
Meditation on Chaos................................................................................. 50
Taraxacum Officinale ("Common Dandelion") ..................................... 51
Ars Musicorum.......................................................................................... 52
The Day We Sang Psalms.......................................................................... 53
Redemption ............................................................................................... 54
Liturgy........................................................................................................ 55
Praise Song for Ants .................................................................................. 56
[learning how the body feels] .................................................................. 57
Poem of Fucking Gratitude ...................................................................... 58

*Acknowledgments* ........................................................................................ 59

*Gratitude* ...................................................................................................... 60

*This book is dedicated to my parents,
who gave me the gift of curiosity,
the ability to find beauty in the smallest of things,
and a love of language.*

*I*

**Elegy for Pre-pandemic Existence**

There are no answers
scattered in the dust
that falls in motes
along the window ledge.

Do you look out the window
to forget? Or to remember
a time not that long ago
when dusk fell
before you could walk
outside to catch it.
When you were free
and the dark was not
your only consolation.

Do you remember days
when the setting sun left you, and
time melted along the horizon
as you walked in long shadows?
Did you feel bereft or reflective?
Your silence came from fatigue,
unlike now, when silence is
the only company you keep,
and, despite the glaring sun,
you live under a constant shadow
that has no choice but to consume
you.

Sit a while longer by the window.
Write your name in the dust.
One day someone will know
you were here.

**the fragrance of your ancestors**

Dear Children,

A metal urn sits on the banks
of the holy river, where we
will all be swallowed.
Churned through time and
outside of it, to become one
again with ourselves.

You have not seen the light
of your first day, and yet
you are here with me today.
Chanting, praying, joining
the ashes of the elders with
the flowing waters.

The sun will rise and set
on me today
and I will think of you.
Just as one day, I hope
you will think of me
and will return to free
my ashes in the water.

I will know on that day
that you are here,
as you stand to chant
your prayers.
I will recognize you by
the fragrance of your ancestors.

Love,
Papa

**Ode to My Grandma's Kitchen Table**

This is for all the egg noodles
left to dry on top of waxed paper
and for all the times my small hand
stole a few before they fell into boiling broth.

This is for all the bowls of oatmeal
for all the onion and butter sandwiches
for all cabbage chopped and celery minced
for all the family gossip consumed
around your laminate edges.

This is for generations of cookies
rolled and cut by hands of all sizes
for sugar and cinnamon dusting
for hot casseroles and trivets
for late night snacks and card games.

This is for all the sorrow you held
for the days when the pantry was empty
for the nights when a bed was still made
for the days filled with peony perfume
for all the scrapes and scars bandaged.

This is for laughter and anger
for snow on one's boots
for hair dropped by your feet
and the quiet buzz of clippers
for cups of Sanka with evaporated milk
for blackberry brandy before bed.

This is for nights where you stood alone
in the quiet of a grieving house
for familial lineages.

This is for life.

**Driving Home**

There is something about the barn
sitting in solitude amid miles of empty fields
sunlight fills the chinks with corn-colored light
brightening a landscape, where everything
is a different shade of grey.

If hope is the thing with feathers
it is nesting in this barn,
having flown from the small stand
of nearby trees—tall and skinny
huddled like self-conscious teens
around the place where the farmhouse stood.

Cars will come and go on this Ohio road
speed past the broken barn without a second
glance, but the barn will watch and keep
count, as it always has.

And the feathery thing will sing
a deep-throated song
leave its downy feathers
to carpet the barn's
cracked earthen floors.

**Anniversary**

*for my parents*

It was a different April 14th.
The bottom of your dress blows forward
and you hold the veil away from your face.
No matter the wind
your smile holds strong.

You and he lean on each other,
his arm on your waist.
He waves. You hold a bouquet.

The wind blows your sister's hat
across the flat green lawn.

Now more than seventy years later
the wind has blown you back
together. Leaning. Laughing.

Today I stand outside in the wind
wondering if I'll find any lace.

## Letter to My Mother in Her Absence

Wading into the miasma of morning,
I smell the heat before I feel
its radiant warmth.

Orange balls of light bounce
into the living room
paint my walls in dawn.

The time change has shifted my day
the light appears earlier
and then disappears too soon.
I am in darkness before my work ends,
which makes me feel both sad and tired.

Leaves are late to find their colors this year.
Their hues light up like fire in the sun
and are the only brightness at day's end.
They contrast against the cool sky.

My dreams have been vivid and real.
They leave my head swimming
in a language I can't touch.
Last night I heard a voice say

>*you were born in the afterlife*

I don't believe it.

Otherwise, I would be sharing a cup
of Constant Comment tea with you,
instead of leaving the pages of this letter
to blow across the pink granite of your name.

**Family Recipe**

There is nothing sacred
about the lemon juice
extracted with bits
of pulp, a random seed,
and added to a family recipe.

But it doesn't belong.

This recipe was born
in a Midwest kitchen,
amid five kids and no money.

Lemon was pie filling or
came in a can, frozen,
stirred into a drink
for hot August afternoons.

Even as it brightens, this lemon
is out of place
for tastebuds accustomed
to the bland,
made by a mother
who was used to creating
the just-one-more meal
from the ordinary bits
found in her cupboard.

**Not Even the Rain**

> *Distill it from the offering/of his hands*
> ~ Shailja Patel, Migritude

In photos, I can guess my father's age
by looking at his hands.

Before the war, he sat and read,
a magazine steady between his two
good hands. He held my mom, arm
around her waist, and smiled broadly,
his gaze just beyond the frame.

After the war, he held my mother tightly,
armed with seven good fingers.
His smile had aged, gaze had softened,
like his palms
which opened to make room
for the five tiny hands
who would come to seek
refuge there.

**Ode to My Older Sister**

The other day, I rode backwards
on the train. I felt disoriented
and panicked when I thought
I had missed my stop.

Which made me think of you,
dear sister, and it sounds corny,
but the idea of life
without you is like that
backwards train ride.

It's not that you are good
at orienteering—your sense
of direction is less than optimal.
It's the idea of navigating alone
that makes me anxious.

I trip and stumble along my beaten path.
You come and lead me off it
every time to a joyous adventure.

And as much as I complain
about your Pollyanna optimism,
you always manage to reach inside me
and massage my heart back to life.

Tomorrow, and the day after, and
the day after that one,
I will still get on that train.
I only ask that the last of those times
we get on board together.
We can enter the tunnel holding hands
and it won't matter if we are lost
on the other side.

**Birthday Poem #26 (for Sam)**

It's rainy and cold this morning,
unlike the morning you were born
when the air was brittle.

You charmed your way into this world
and in the flash of an eye
here you are in full bloom.

You once told me that you chose
to be born in our family.
I chuckled at your imagination.
But now I'm not so sure.
Some days it feels like you waded
through the stars to seed yourself
inside me.

You're made of light and dreams
and old-world wisdom.
There are days when you outshine the sun
yet you remember to be humble.

Your feet are mostly on the ground
yet your spirit wanders
through other worlds.
I sometimes fear it won't return.

Someone once said that you're magic.
You built a home that rests inside you,
grown from the land, the ancestors, and love.
It's all the magic you'll ever need.

**Journey**

> *A mythic journey begins with a well packed van.*
> *While Atlas carried the world on his shoulders,*
> *fortunately, we have a luggage carrier.*

In the morning, our van is packed,
Sam grants the cats one last scratch,
the house alarm is armed and ready.

When we descend to the city's edge,
Sam declares before the bridge,
"I will only cross this river once,"
meaning that he will not return.

Now it's miles of macadam
lined with firs and sunflowers
that turn with time
and watch us pass.

We drive through Virginia, North
Carolina, our appetites
not sated by the burgers we eat in the car.
We have many rivers yet to cross.

Atlanta seems like a mythic island;
Louisiana, another planet.
I think we will wander this ocean
of roads forever.

I check the maps again.

It's strange to think how empty
the return trip will be,
like Charon and his ferry—
passage only guaranteed one way—
and I, like Demeter, will
barter for a temporary return.
Eat all the luscious red
fruit you want my child.
Be careful of the seeds.

**Brotherly Love**

The music that is more bass than melody
blares into the back seat and fills my ears with words,
swirls around my brain and distracts me
from my reading but I don't ask to turn it off.

I watch the clouds outside the window
remain steady as everything else rushes by.

Even though this music leaves me
wedged between generations,
wedged among boxes, pillows, bags,
I don't want to interrupt the moment.

This is a moment of brothers.

A moment of the two young men driving the van
and their excitement.
It's a moment I've wanted all their lives.

This is my life now:
my sons in the front seat,
steering my path down an unknown
road, bonding over something
I don't completely understand.

The youngest one is at the wheel,
the older one is navigating.
Dad is asleep. I try to read.
Isn't this really the next phase of life?
The adventure of college,
the emptiness at home,
the music I cannot enter?

These boys are oblivious.
They continue with their music and maps,
watching the clouds gather on the road ahead.

Meanwhile, I have to surrender to the beat
of the music, even if I don't understand it.

It's the beat of brotherly love.

## Art Therapy

my therapist says I am made of steel
it feels more like steel wool
wound around and around
abrasive, tangled, messy

my therapist says I am steel yet soft
it feels more like covered in glass—
strong at the core, but fragile,
easily shattered, cracked in places

my therapist says humans have enormous
capacity to find beauty in the world
it feels like an obsidian mountain to climb
with a stone necklace its only reward

my therapist says by humans I mean you,
says I find beauty in the smallest places
it feels like I want to unclench
my jaw, my body, my heart

my therapist says go
find yourself in the world,
appreciate the mark you've made,
see how much you and beauty
have in common

*II*

# Sovereignty

*after Ha Jin*

I am holding my quiet center
which brims like an ocean oracle.
I walk alone in an obsidian canyon.

I am holding and waiting
for the ghost mist to clear.
I don't know if I am strong
or stubborn or stupid.

I must hold my quiet center,
even as you are so distant
and foolish.
My perseverance feels like
a stone mountain:
too rough to climb
too solid to ignore.

I will hold quietly to my center
with my friend, Solitude, and
wait for the shadow to pass.
I will inhale the galaxy
and begin to turn.

**[what is the difference]**

what is the difference
between
loneliness and solitude

one a yawning chasm
the other a peaceful valley

you have to choose
which side of the glass
to drink from

**Reflection**

Abandoned, isolated,
no sense of purpose,
Time blows through me
like leaves on the sidewalk.
I am a living memorial
that spirits visit
in commemoration
of what once existed.
I find rose petals at my feet.

**Ode to Dead Skin Cells**

parchment paper
coded with my life
DNA floating
imperceptible to the eye

a speck of me
everywhere I go
spread across the city
or even the world

where will the wind
blow me today

## The Jade Belt

I feel the scales form.
First behind my ears
next along ridges of bone
between shoulder blades.

The doctors say it's a rash.
I disagree.

I see how the scales shimmer
feel how they seek warmth.
I am transforming.

There's a Chinese folk tale
about a greedy man who dies.
Before he returns to Earth
he's given a choice of clothing.
He finds a glittering suit
with a belt of translucent jade.
He returns as a golden snake
striped green along its back.
His wishes turn sideways, like the way
he now moves.

The doctors say medicine will heal me,
make the scales disappear and soften
the leathery skin forming on my body.

I palm the pills.
Pray.
Please, I whisper, let me be
a creature that shimmers in the night.

**Feral**

I put on makeup
to remind me that I am not lost.

I am not a child of the pandemic
returned to feral roots.

Charcoal black lines my eyes
pink shades the curve of cheekbones.

Lips drip red
like blood.

I cannot seem to tame
my desire for flesh.

**Juggling Scimitars**

In a fit of sleeplessness
I realize that I have moved
from anxiety to resignation.

Knives no longer hollow me.

I've reached some kind of truce
with ambiguity.

I don't know if
this dreamless state
is called insomnia or silence
but I'll drink
from its cup of inky calm
and listen for the sound of metal
hitting the floor around me.

**Chaos Theory**

my mind is an asteroid belt
swirling with meteors of memory
comet tails of creativity
chaos theory at its best
all the cacophony quieted
by the vacuum of the Milky Way

## The Weight of It All

Grief grows stronger
as days dwindle by.

We feel the dead walk closer to us,
exhale leaves from their throats.

Grief pours down in golden rays
in the afternoon light,
hangs through bare branches.

We watch Grief shape shift like clouds
racing and returning for days.

What we see is what Grief carries:
all that once was
all that lies ahead.

We burn candles,
to bring in the light, otherwise
we would collapse
from the weight of it all.

**Anniversary Poem**

thoughts of you run through me
like atmospheric rivers
drown my heart with sorrow
please throw me a life jacket

**Bad Habits**

I fell in the hole again

no one notices
I drag myself out

the hole is wholly imaginary
it follows me and traps me

there I go again

sometimes I fall deeper
        faster
                longer

sometimes I can't get out

stupid hole

why do you know my name

**from the ashes**

when the heart is too heavy to carry
open the latches of your ribs
empty your sorrows with a bucket
let your lungs breathe kindness
inhale the sweetness of sunrise,
the promise of stars
exhale the grudges you harbor
along with the disappointments
allow yourself to feel flutters
like tiny birds in your chest
this is your heart unburdening,
stretching its wings
you will experience lightness
you may grow feathers
know that you are not broken
allow yourself to soar

**Self Portrait in 10 Lines**

Crows chattering at the end of the day
Four books on the table with bookmarks halfway through
Hydrangea blossoms with dark pink, blue, and purple petals
Cats in the window by the front door
An empty bag of Cajun french fries
One sip of coffee in the bottom of a candy cane mug
Pens of every color lined up in a drawer
True crime podcasts
A single red sunflower in a field of yellow
The glow of a full moon through the window

**Jean Cocteau's Orpheus**

If Death
travels back
and forth
through the mirror,
how
will anyone
remember
our true name,
when the mouth
moves with no sound?

**Chaos**

Try to tease meaning
out of impermanence—
random candy wrappers,
a plastic cup blown
down the alley.

How do you count blessings?

**Grace**
*~for Moira*

you are ache and groan and pain and breath
you know your body's grace but not its poise

you are groan and ache and dizzy
you are space and tired and pain
you do not seem to know this body
as if it were temporary shelter

you live, you flourish, you struggle,
you cry on your shadow's shoulder

you are beatitudes,
find strength in weakness
light in darkness
this is your greatest teaching

no matter the broken pieces, the loss,
the cracks, the challenge of opening
your eyes one more day, of taking
one step or raising a hand
in surrender

grace floods you
fills the cracks, but doesn't heal

there is grace in imperfection
there is grace in longing
in the daily habits that move you
from place to place

it is not your knowledge that liberates,
but this daily movement through
the pain, the cracks, the miasma
into the grace of you

**[where is the difference]**

where is the difference
between grief and anguish?

it's in the curl of "g"
the body
stricken, crumpled
unable to raise itself

## Poem With a Line from Sherwin Bitsui

*No one questioned the sand anymore.*

Also, no one spoke to the ocean.
We forgot to care
about the stories they held
or we just didn't listen.

When the super blue blood moon rose
we were all inside ourselves.
I saw it through the trees,
tried to walk toward it,
but the sirens held me back.

It rose and set with all its wisdom,
while we ate and slept in ordinary time.

No one questioned the sand,
nor the hourglass,
nor the days that slid by us.

One day we awoke
to tapping on the windows.
I did not want to see
the bony hand of Death
pointing or beckoning.
I left the curtains pulled.

**Blue Friday or the Bluest Blue**

I got the Blues so bad
my eyes are invisible

I got the Blues so bad
people think I'm a river

I got the Blues so bad
I have constellations on my back

I got the Blues so bad
every day feels like the day after Christmas

I got the Blues so bad
the other colors are jealous

I got the Blues so bad
Muddy Waters sounds cheerful

I got the Blues so bad
Melancholy is my new roommate

I got the Blues so bad
I only have sky and more sky

I got the Blues so bad
my feet are cement blocks

I got the Blues so bad
my mouth is an iron gate

I got the Blues so bad
my hair has turned to snakes

I got the Blues so bad
clouds drift through me

I got the Blues so bad
weeping angels console me

I got the Blues so bad
trees drop their leaves as I pass

I got the Blues so bad
the blue jay lost his voice

I got the Blues so bad
Day won't get up

I got the Blues so bad
the moon half smiles at me

I got the Blues so bad

I got the Blues so bad

I got the Blues so bad
even my pen's ink understands

**Resilience**

Even the "R" has curves
bends to the ground
rebounds
joins the others
to lead the way
on its thin legs

**Catharsis**

Days are hard to gauge.
Time winds ribbons around us
in frayed spirals.

Amazement arrives in small packages:
a ground pine poking through dead leaves,
snowy white birch limbs splayed along the trail,
the crisp line of darkness along the ridge at twilight.

Release comes gradually.

It's not the satisfaction
of smashed plates, ripped photos,
or even a scream in the woods.

It's more settled.
It grows slowly,
bathes us in soft fall color
as we remember how to breathe.

**The Sun is an Insomniac**

The sun is an insomniac
up earlier every day,
bouncing balls of light
through the windows
as coffee brews.

In evening, the sun refuses
to lay down quietly, instead
it rouses cardinals and robins
to scratch for seeds and crumbs,
sends low-flung beams
to ricochet on walls
long after dinner.

Some say the sun never sleeps,
just creeps from house to house
to light up cob-webbed corners
and stirs the creatures
it seeks for companions.

**Life is Beautiful**

I have a tiny Pollyanna
hiding deep inside me.
She sees good everywhere.
She believes the world to be
a beautiful, happy place.
I know she isn't real,
but I don't tell her.
I don't want to hurt
her tiny tender feelings.

**Beeswax**

Buddha's wax head smiles
even as the wick burns,
his forehead melting
over his third eye.

He smiles as the warm liquid
coats his eyes and the soft
edges of his ears fold
onto themselves.

Even as the wax drips along
the corners of his mouth,
he seems to say

*Remember nothing stays.*

A solitary bee, maybe the last of the season,
comes to the window and cleans itself.
He nods to the candle in recognition,
the hard work of his summer over.
Then like the waxen figure, the bee melts
away into the fall sun.

**The Way**

The footsteps you followed
end abruptly.

A friend once told you
it's a jungle out there
and now you have no clear path.

Sometimes a vision is in your head;
sometimes it's in your feet.

Close your eyes and listen.
Your feet will know
where to make your way.

*III*

**In Praise of the Vaccine**

In a world
where every task
feels like
it takes
an Act of God

you slip in like
a double agent

tiny
invisible

you infiltrate
unknown territory

silent
stealthy
you slip the code
into the body

you are not welcomed
and warnings of
your entrance spread
like fire in the blood

but then your identity
unmasked
your code, not enemy
but defense

the body goes back to routine
while you and your spies
keep watch around
the perimeter.

## Chaos II

Everywhere I look: chaos.
Dandelions have taken over,
weeds are knee high
in all directions.
I cannot tell if the rustle
of leaves is the wind or
the grackle searching for dinner
and nesting twigs.
Nothing is what it seems tonight.
The soil I thought was perfect
hides pockets of red clay and pebbles.
Even the bumble bee seems confused.
Evening breezes play enchanted notes
on the porch chimes, the sun burrows
farther into the earth's edge,
and I am left sorting shoots
to determine what should remain.

## Enter and Exit Singing

      I.
Back and forth
the golden orb swings.
The earth spins.
The golden orb does not count,
does not age. Time is nothing to it.

      II.
What is time?
Stasis

      III.
The sleeping princess awakens
from a hundred years' dream
where little has changed.
We don't know the side effects
of enchantment.
Her dreams, her prince, her world
tunnels its way out of the roots.

      IV.
The golden orb continues to pass
the shadow is cast.
Discs go flat
to catch the sun's light.

      V.
What is time?
Metamorphosis
Awakening

      VI.
The periodical cicada, that orange-eyed
sleeping beauty of the insect world,
emerges from under the long shadow
of time's pendulum.
One night, 17 years.
They awaken singing.
No digging, no hives, no anything.

VII.
How long is a night?
a decade
a century
a pandemic

VIII.
We will awaken and emerge one day.
Grope our way out,
the husk of this pandemic
a shadow on the floor.

IX.

The earth spins
the pendulum makes another pass.

X.

Let us walk with the princess atop the wall of night.
Let us look up now and then, look in the trees and sing.
Let us remember the cicada's hot pursuit of connection
before time runs out again.

Let us gaze at our reflections in that golden orb,
make the most of brilliant days between darkness,
always enter and exit singing.

**Awakening**

your body stiffens as it settles
air quiets down where dust motes land.

the earth warms to you
and you feel safe.

what is time—an hour,
a week, a millennium—all the same.

if you were entombed in a cave
who would roll away the stone?

what do miracles look like to you?

>    a single dandelion in a field
>    pink clouds at dawn
>    a blue jay feather

after many seasons your body
begins to unsettle.

can you recognize your beauty
as you awaken?

shed your protective husk
feel sunlight lift your pallor.

allow yourself to emerge fully
the world awaits your song.

## Meditation on Chaos

where does tranquility exist
the garden thrives on chaos, wild seeds floating in wind
or planted by bird droppings, detritus of squirrel snacks
chaos of the mind is a different animal
the mind chatters wildly, like a troop of chimps
in the middle of grooming, loudly ricochets
down rabbit holes of distraction, memory, dreams
the mind refuses to be tamed as it wishes to be tamed
a conundrum, an enigma, a roadblock

## Taraxacum Officinale ("Common Dandelion")

Dandelion, there is nothing
common about you.

Yellowest of yellow
tinged orange, like yolks.
A shorn lawn
your canvas
you paint tiny suns
across the green grass sky.

Bees rely on you
children adore you
many a nose yellowed
because of your sweet scent.

Magician
you disappear
reappear transformed
puffball, delicate
clock of seeds
holder of wishes
gone in a gust
or the sigh of breath.

**Ars Musicorum**

there is music in silence
and the tiniest bird song

layer upon layer of sound

the murmur of a purr
the scratch of a pen
the forgiveness of the paper

## The Day We Sang Psalms

on the morning Peter died
the hospice nurse woke us
shortly after dawn

said she heard
the word *death*
as he exhaled

we gathered on his bed
nestled in the heavy rattle
of his breathing

the room was dark
then a single ray of sun
brightened one corner

the corner where he watched
watched as if he knew
knew what waited there

we sang a song he wrote
sang with every cell in our bodies
every memory we ever held

the light beam spread across the ceiling
as if a piece of sky had opened
and beckoned Peter toward it

and we sang to him
and he watched the light
and our voices lifted him higher

and higher
and off he went
and he became the light

we held that last empty note
high and soft until
the light disappeared

**Redemption**

If you wish to speak
of what is holy,
you must begin
with the body.

The body:
imperfect flesh
where the sacred resides.

Put skin on your gods,
for even they know
every crack,
every scar,
allows our divinity
to be present.

**Liturgy**

the trees are your saints
throw open the doors
let the birds be your choir
sink into the soul of the earth

no sin here is unforgivable
confession is not necessary
the ravens know and absolve you

the wind is an act of contrition
the rain is prayer

life feeds life feeds life
an eternity exists in a fern frond

**Praise Song for Ants**

Praise the tiny black ants.
Praise their resilience
to be knocked down, drowned out,
killed, trampled, worn to nothing
and then to bloom again.
Praise the ants who insist on finding a way inside
through hairline crack or gaping crevice. Praise their
strength, their fortitude in finding
that last crumb of bread or the sticky
syrup of fruit juice on the floor. Praise
their skill at moving every part and parcel
of a nest when a pitchfork upends them
in spring. Praise the teamwork of
carrying six times their weight over
and over again while seeking shelter.
Praise their ability to disappear and
reappear so quickly. Praise their queen
in her fertility and the workers in
their loyalty. Praise their multitudes, their pathways,
their ant mounds, their single-mindedness.
Praise their force of nature for showing
me time and again how little
of this world belongs to me.

## [learning how the body feels]

learning how the body feels
one movement to the next
what is bone
what is muscle
how to move inside
the tiniest movements
here is the pelvis
here is the tail bone
here is a femur
here is a shoulder blade
one muscle extends
another one contracts
and all the while
you breathe

    in

          out

                in

out


a space opens
for you to step out

## Poem of Fucking Gratitude

*for Persis K*

Today is the free day on my cursing diet, so
I have to write this poem of fucking gratitude.

Gratitude because this morning the sky
is a goddamned beautiful bodacious blue,
so clear that you can see into forever.

Gratitude because the music on the radio
is so damned cheerful that it makes me want to dance,
makes me feel the closest to joy I have felt in months.

Gratitude because of all the goddamned poets
who bleed their words onto pages and write
their damned souls out every day, just to bring
some fucking beauty into this shitty world,
just to speak some fucking truth in this world
full of alternate facts. I love them and they are my kin.

Gratitude because sometimes on a day like today,
you have to be fucking grateful, because
the sky can be so fucking blue and the music so damn happy.

Gratitude because sometimes you have to open
the floodgates of your heart to the goddamned shitty world,
in order to see who you really fucking are.

*Acknowledgments*

I am grateful to the following publications, where these poems found their first home, sometimes in a slightly different form:

*After Enchantment*: "Driving Home"

*Blue Heron Review*: "Beeswax"

*Burgeon Press*: "Blue Friday or the Bluest Blue"

*Dear Vaccine: Global Voices Speak to the Pandemic*, The Kent State University Press: "In Praise of the Vaccine"

*Enchantment of the Ordinary,* Mutabilis Press: "Praise Song for Ants"

*Little Patuxent Review*: "Not Even the Rain"

*The Mid-Atlantic Review*: "Resilience," "The Jade Belt"

*Mikemaggio.net/April 2021*: "Enter and Exit Singing"

*The Orchards Poetry Journal*: "Letter to My Mother in Her Absence"

*The Southern Quill*: "The Weight of It All"

*Washington Writers Publishing House*: "Sovereignty"

*Gratitude*

They say it takes a village to raise a child. I would say the same for writing and compiling a collection of poems. There are those who inspire, those who mentor and guide you along the path, those who cheer from the sidelines, and those who are willing to quietly pick you up when you fall apart. I am grateful to all those who are part of my "poetic" village, specifically, and in no particular order:

thanks to my writing partner and comrade-in-arms, Regie Cabico, for keeping my pen on the page, for supporting me through all the darkness, for making me laugh during hard times, and for not giving up;

thanks to Michael Gushue for editorial honesty and gentleness, mentorship, encouragement, and decades of friendship;

thanks to Larry Joseph for helping to think through themes, flow, and for continued positivity and general excitement;

thanks to my sister, Skeeter, who has been my inspiration, taskmaster, instigator, and critical reader for most of my life;

thanks to Moira Dougherty and Kat Tanaka for their proofreading prowess;

thanks to The Porches Writing Retreat for giving me a week of beautiful sunrises and the space to begin this book and special thanks to the DC Commission on the Arts and Humanities for the Arts & Humanities Fellowship grant that made this work possible;

thanks to the vibrant DC poetry community and those who have sustained me over the years, especially Sarah Browning, Carmen Calatayud, Grace Cavalieri, Teri Ellen Cross Davis, Dwayne Lawson-Brown, Peter Montgomery, Kim Roberts, Joseph Ross, and Dan Vera;

thanks to all the friends and co-workers who have read, commented, and otherwise influenced and encouraged my work;

thanks to you, dear reader, for allowing my poems into your heart and your home;

and last, but not least, thanks to those who have always had faith in me, particularly my husband and two sons.

**Susan Scheid** was born and raised in Lima, Ohio, a place that allowed her vivid imagination to wander through the cornfields and natural landscapes. Scheid came to poetry early in life when her father read her poems at bedtime. Her interest was fed by the stories he recounted about reading poetry to the other wounded soldiers in the army hospitals of World War II. Scheid honed her craft while working for the last 30 years as a legal secretary. In addition to poetry, Scheid has pursued artistic endeavors as an adult student of modern dance at Dance Place and ballet at Washington Ballet School, and continues to feed that passion every year at the Noyes School of Rhythm in Connecticut. Scheid's first book, *After Enchantment*, was inspired by beloved fairy tale characters. Her poetry has appeared most recently in *Poetry X Hunger, Washington Writers Publishing House, The Southern Quill, Blue Heron Review, The MidAtlantic Review*, as well as *The Orchards Press, Burgeon Press, About Place Journal, Gargoyle, Truth to Power, Beltway Poetry Quarterly, Little Patuxent Review, The Sligo Journal, Silver Birch Press, Tidal Basin Review*, and other journals. Her work is also included in the anthologies *Poetic Art, Enchantment of the Ordinary*, and *Dear Vaccine: Global Voices Speak to the Pandemic*. She has been a featured poet at Sunday Kind of Love, as well as a regular at the open mic. Additionally, Scheid has been featured on multiple occasions at La-Ti-Do, Takoma Park Third Thursday, The Reach at the Kennedy Center, and at venues in Ohio, Texas, and Louisiana. Scheid served as a reader for the Split This Rock Annual Poetry Contest and as a judge for the Parkmont Poetry Festival, both housed in DC. In addition to writing and reading poetry, Scheid has taught workshops for Split this Rock, as well as for BAWA/Brookland Arts. Scheid was Artist in Residence at the Noyes School of Rhythm for two years, where she blended writing workshops with movement and visual art. Scheid served on the Board of Directors for Split This Rock and as its co-chair, where she brought poetry and activism to many people across the country. She currently resides with her cat and dog in the Brookland neighborhood of Washington, DC.

Instagram: susankscheid
Facebook: Susan Kay Scheid
www.susanscheid.com

www.ingramcontent.com/pod-product-compliance
Lightning Source LLC
Chambersburg PA
CBHW030058170426
43197CB00010B/1572